To

_____

From

_____

Date

_____

WINNING THOUGHTS

- with Real Stories from the Mission Field -

A 31-Day Devotional for Developing
a Winning Mindset

Stacy Egbo

THE
CORNERSTONE
P U B L I S H I N G

WINNING THOUGHTS

A 31-Day Devotional for Developing a Winning Mindset

Copyright © 2020 by **Stacy Egbo**

ISBN: 978-1-952098-09-3

Cornerstone Publishing

A Division of Cornerstone Creativity Group LLC
Phone: +1(516) 547-4999
info@thecornerstonepublishers.com
www.thecornerstonepublishers.com

To order bulk copies of this book or to contact the author please email: stacyegbo@gmail.com

CONTENTS

ACKNOWLEDGMENTS

Every day of my life, I stand in awe of the great God, who left everything He could be doing, to create me. I am the second of over 23 children. I could have given up on life at any time but God kept me. So, when I say, THANK YOU LORD, it's not just a routine statement. God, You are my everything and I love you so much.

Special thanks to my family and my siblings. You are my bedrock, the foundation of everything I do. I appreciate the only living parent I have, Igwe Patrick Ifoh. May God keep you to see all your children's children to the third generation.

A special shout out to my friends and spiritual siblings. I can't mention all your names because this page will not be enough.

To Cornerstone Publishing and Pastor Gbenga Showunmi, thank you for believing in me and for seeing this project through my eyes.

To my extraordinary DBMM (Divine Benevolence

WINNING THOUGHTS: A 31-DAY DEVOTIONAL

Medical Mission) team, I love you all so much. What a joy it's been for me to travel and do ministry with you all!

I am particularly grateful to Pastor Steve Soyebo, Pastor Sam Hunsu, Dr. Wole Oladute, Emen Washington, Daniel Jones, and my son John-Patrick (JP) Egbo, for being my unofficial editors, lol. I throw things at you all and you still catch them with positive feedback and encouragement.

To everyone who ever doubted that they could start something and hope to finish, this is for you. Thank you and keep pushing!

FOREWORD

The Bible speaks often about the power of the mind and our thoughts. Winning is one of the most important things in life, and thoughts are very important in determining our actions and ultimately our lifestyle. To put the "winning" in our thoughts leads to a lifestyle that maximizes our potential and (most importantly) reflects the image of our Creator, God.

If you change the way you think, it changes your perspective, which changes how you act in the world. The central theme of Jesus' first sermon in Matthew 4:17 is changing the way you think and act, to the right way. It says, *"From that time Jesus began to preach and to say, "Repent, for the kingdom of heaven is at hand" (NKJV).*

Jesus challenged people to change their thinking because, regardless of how many times you read through the Bible, if you don't change your thinking (renew your mind), you will simply impose your prejudices over what you are reading.

Amongst my many God-given assignments is the mission work which has given me the opportunity to meet different people and visit many countries and churches. From these experiences, the Lord has drawn my attention to one of the least understood aspects of the Christian life: Power of intimate relationship with God. Coming boldly to the throne of grace brings tremendous blessings, as stated in Hebrews 4:16, *"Let us therefore come boldly to the throne of grace, that we may obtain mercy and find grace to help in time of need"* (NKJV)

Unfortunately, many are missing out on blessings from a devotional lifestyle with God. Among many important benefits from studying with a Spirit-filled devotional is that "thing" that evokes God's presence to help one think more clearly about God and his miraculous ways.

My connection and interaction with the "exuberant", "full of life" Minister Stacy Egbo in life and ministry is not just one of a long time friend, but one of ministers ministering together to the needs of the underprivileged wherever the Lord leads on this earthly realm. On some of our various medical mission trips, which included many medical practitioners, God highlighted Minister Stacy's gifting in other areas of ministry as it is now expressed, as a way of highlighting the rationale or "angle" of this devotional book.

Min. Stacy Egbo's devotional, *Winning Thoughts,* is more like having a date with Jesus Himself. This devotional is a plea to embrace winning thoughts as a means of fulfilling God's plans for our lives. It is a plea to reject spiritual degradation by safeguarding your heart and embracing divine thoughts, leading to living a wholesome life in Christ Jesus. It is a plea to see meditation on God's word as a necessary, God-ordained means of knowing Him. As Joshua 1:8 says, *"This Book of the Law shall not depart from your mouth, but you shall meditate in it day and night, that you may observe to do according to all that is written in it. For then you will make your way prosperous, and then you will have good success."*

Winning Thoughts shows you how to engage the Scriptures and apply it to real-life experiences. Your thoughts are an important means of fueling the knowledge of God to lead to immediate expression of reverence before the Lord and service to the world. *"Finally, brethren, whatever things are true, whatever things are noble, whatever things are just, whatever things are pure, whatever things are lovely, whatever things are of good report, if there is any virtue and if there is anything praiseworthy—meditate on these things."* (Philippians 4:8, NKJV)

For "winning thoughts", Choose God!

Pastor Steve O. Soyebo
House on the Word Ministry

I have known Minister Stacy Egbo for many years. She loves God and she loves people. I have had the privilege of having her join us on many mission trips. She is so passionate about medical and evangelical outreaches on the mission field. She has never looked back since her first outreach with us to Brazil in 2006. She is also a devoted worship leader and gospel artiste. She loves to encourage those who are discouraged, and support the poor and the orphans at every opportunity.

This daily devotional highlights her experiences and passion for all that she loves. Reading the testimonies in the devotional reminds me of the power of God to heal, to save and to deliver from all afflictions. This devotional should motivate you to be more active and live out your faith. Like iron that sharpens iron, let us all be inspired to serve the Lord wholeheartedly like Minister Stacy.

Dr. Wole Oladute
Medical Doctor, St Luke's medical Center
Founder, Divine Benevolence medical Missions

AUTHOR'S PREFACE

People always ask me, "What keeps you going? Why are you always excited and joyful, full of life?" Here is the answer: *winning thoughts.* I have always separated my emotions from what is real. What is real is that I am loved. I am a Christian woman. I was fearfully and wonderfully made. I am a victor, not a victim. I am cherished and wanted by God. I am His prized possession. He has given me joy, which no one can take away. When I remember these, I daily choose this countenance that everyone sees.

I do have challenges that should weigh me down. I do go through trials and tribulations. But I have discovered that a winning thought can transform your mindset and give you a boost to get you through the day. This is why I am the cheerful, exuberant, passionate and hilarious Stacy Egbo you see every day.

You, too, can win in every situation of life, in every challenge life throws at you. My son was almost wrongfully thrown into prison in America but the winning thought I had was: "We are the Redeemed of the Lord and we have been ransomed by the blood of Christ. We are victorious and we can never lose." And, of course, the Lord saw us through. What gets you through the day? Add that to your daily winning thoughts and, together with this devotional, you will come out winning.

This devotional was birthed out of my experiences on the medical mission field. So, you will find, in it, a combination of Scripture passages - simple, short, yet powerful – and real life testimonies from the mission field that will further show you the wonder-working power of our God. These stories are like immune-boosters that will bump up your spiritual immune system to bring you to the winning side. They are like daily vitamins - take them for 31 days and you will become spiritually healthy and ready to conquer anything that the world throws at you. Tell yourself again, "I am winning!" Yes, because you are!

I'm delighted to say that the best part of my mission trips always and forever will be the morning devotions. Oh, I love it when we gather to pray, read the word and find strength to face the mission for the day. It's where we share testimonies and prayer points and laugh at ourselves. I hope as you read this daily, you can see that nothing is impossible for God to do. He's a miracle-working God and He loves His people.

Yes, you can go on a mission trip; yes, you can serve on the mission field! There's no qualification except to love God and love people. Don't worry about how and when; just trust God to help make your heart desire come true. If there's any way I can help you on this journey, please reach out to me. My contact details are below.

Follow us on all social media platforms. I love you so much. May God bless you, keep you, make His face shine upon you and be gracious to you always. Amen!

Connect with me:

Facebook: Stacy Nkem Egbo
IG: stacyegbo
YouTube: stacyegbo

DAY 1

STARTING OVER

Bible Reading

"Jesus came and told his disciples, "I have been given all authority in heaven and on earth. Therefore, go and make disciples of all the nations, baptizing them in the name of the Father and the Son and the Holy Spirit."
—Matthew 28:18-19

Winning Thoughts

Winners ask the question, "What is in my hand?" or "What ability do I possess?" Use it before your hands get empty again. Use it and watch God multiply your efforts. Use what's been given and don't be afraid of trying.

Mission Field Testimony

The first time I saw her, I prejudged her. She had fake eyelashes and long nails, and was dressed like a prostitute. Yeah, I had seen them in so many places. When she approached me, I had a self-righteous attitude but the nurse in me kicked in once I saw her left arm. It was swollen and secured with a scarf. I tried touching it but she winced in pain, pulling back. I asked what happened to her arm. She told me it had been broken by another woman who had beaten her.

After triage, I asked if we could pray for her, while she waited to see the doctor. She objected. "Whenever people pray, they push people down," she said. I laughed and promised we would not do that to her. "We are not those kind of people," I assured her." She agreed for a short prayer but as soon as the pastor started praying for her, she fell on the floor. She shook and screamed and, after about three minutes, became quiet.

When she opened her eyes and asked to be let up, she was completely transformed. She took her eyelashes out and wept, asking God to forgive her. We led her to Christ and she was set free.

After that day, she followed us everywhere we went, changed her dressing and cleaned herself up. She became our interpreter and has been serving God ever since. All (Yes, all!) the village people got saved in the next couple of days we were in there. They told us, "If she could be saved and transformed, we want the same God in our lives." Hallelujah!

God has mandated us to go to the world and set the captives free and that's what we must do.

Today's Prayer

Dear God, all I want is to serve you with the little you have given me. I trust you to take care of the rest. Help me to see people the way you see them. Amen.

Further Bible Reading: Matthew 28.

Day 2

SONGS OF VICTORY

Bible Reading

"When they saw the star, they were filled with joy! They entered the house and saw the child with his mother, Mary, and they bowed down and worshiped him. Then they opened their treasure chests and gave him gifts of gold, frankincense, and myrrh." —Matthew 2:10-11

Winning Thought

Joy unspeakable, peace unstoppable, love unchangeable - it all belongs to me. (I love singing, by the way). Joy, joy, joy…it all belongs to me.

Pursue joy! A winning heart has joy. It might not be happiness and excitement and giddiness - just joy, deep in your soul. In the place where that joy is found lies your strength. It's called the joy of the Lord; it only comes from Christ. And since the world didn't give to you, it certainly can't take it away.

Mission Field Testimonies

We had gone to South Africa to help conduct HIV/AIDS tests in a rural village, outside Johannesburg. When we got there, the villagers refused to come out to be tested. They believed that medical tests were often tampered with, leading to wrong diagnoses being given to innocent people.

We tried to convince them to get tested, letting them know that was the only way they could receive free treatments. After that, we waited and waited but they refused to come out.

Suddenly – and apparently prompted by the Holy Spirit – I found myself singing. And, as if on cue, everyone else burst into songs of joy. We used the medicine bottles and different medical supplies to make music. I still remember that, as we sang, I opened my eyes at one point and saw a few extra feet joining us in the circle we had made. Gradually, the feet grew larger in number. Before we knew it, the villagers had all come out and, at the end of that day, we had tested over 120 people.

By the end of our three-day mission, we had tested over 300 people. We were able to assist those who tested positive to get treatment and medications. Glory to God!

Today's Prayer

Thank you, Lord, for you are our healer and protector, even when we are so vulnerable. We ask for your unending joy to fill our hearts and soul. We thank you because you can take care of everything that we can't take care of. Amen.

Further Bible Reading: Matthew 22 and 23.

Day 3

HUMILITY IS NOT MEDIOCRITY

Bible Reading

"Oh, the joys of those who do not follow the advice of the wicked, or stand around with sinners, or join in with mockers. But they delight in the law of the Lord, meditating on it day and night. They are like trees planted along the riverbank, bearing fruit each season. Their leaves never wither, and they prosper in all they do." —Psalm 1:1-3

Winning Thought

To be a winner, you must be firm and assertive. Humility is not mediocrity. Winners take a stand even when others run away. It's not pride, it's not ego, it's not being aggressive.

We must make good use of the time we've been given. A winner cannot walk with scoffers, but if you find yourself amongst them, learn how to correct them wisely or walk away. Do the right thing at the right time. That's the winning attitude.

Mission Field Testimony

He had HIV and AIDS, and they had told him he was dying. We were in one of the main cities in Guyana. The whole village knew he had AIDS and everyone stayed away from him. No one wanted to talk to him. He walked alone on the streets. We had been doing street evangelism, when we met him. He told us his story, expecting us to walk away just like the others, but we stayed.

When the man of God praying for him touched him, he was very shocked. He started crying. He told us that people never touched him, much less hugged him. They were obviously scared of contracting the disease. We all hugged him and prayed some more. We declared healing over him.

Watching us nearby was a young woman who had recently given birth. She was with her baby and her family; and as we attended to the sick man, they were all watching us. There and then she decided on her own to give her life to Christ. We prayed with her and her family. That day, two lives were transformed and we know that the work of God continued in their lives.

Nothing is impossible with God. All you need do is ask Him and then wait for His answer. This might be all you need to surrender everything to Him today.

Today's Prayer

Jesus, I want to be saved. Come into my heart and save me. I repent of my sins and I ask you to cleanse me from all unrighteousness. Restore me and write my name in the Lamb's Book of Life. Amen.

Further Bible Reading: Romans 12 and 13.

Day 4

CRYING IS GOOD

Bible Reading

"And this same God who takes care of me will supply all your needs from his glorious riches, which have been given to us in Christ Jesus." —*Philippians 4:19*

Winning Thought

Winners cry a lot! You say what? Yes, yes, winners are emotional beings. They are not afraid to be vulnerable. It's that part that makes them human. To be a winner, you must be human and be open to pain and attacks. Go to your closet and cry as much as you want; it's a super cleanser - you will see how refreshing it can be - and then wipe your face and runny nose and go face the world again. God is with you and for you!

Mission Field Testimony

We were in Botswana and had visited a small village there to see patients during our medical mission. We went with a good amount of supplies. It was enough - or so we had believed. We quickly set up and started seeing patients. It was almost evening and we had thought the day was coming to a good end.

Then we saw them coming, from everywhere. A woman had used her car to go bring sick people from other villages. Before we knew what was happening, we had become overwhelmed with lots of people to care for. We still managed to see them but we ran out of medications. As we packed to go, the people who couldn't get medications kept begging us to stay and not leave them. They wanted us to take care of them and give them medications before we could go but we explained that we had none left.

We entered our van and started driving off but the villagers started throwing stones at us. One of the young men with us began to cry. He asked, "Why are we leaving? Why can't we find medications from somewhere to give them? Why don't we have enough medications?"

It was heart-wrenching to watch him and to watch the people as they chased after us, following our van to the outskirts of the village. I can never forget their faces, the desperation, the fear, the need. Of course, we had to send someone back there to ensure that their medication needs were met; but it was a good learning process for all of us. Now, in our present trips, we over-plan. Most times, we always have excess medications, so we cannot run out, all by God's grace and mercy.

Today's Prayer

Lord, your grace is more than enough for us. Your mercy is from everlasting to everlasting. You are the God of abundance; please, supply all our needs according to your riches in glory by Christ Jesus. Amen.

Further Bible Reading: Philippians 3 and 4.

DAY 5

TRUE PURITY

Bible Reading

"Don't just pretend to love others. Really love them. Hate what is wrong. Hold tightly to what is good."
— *Romans 12:9*

Winning Thought

Winners defend the poor and the unjustly treated, without being defensive themselves. Don't try to be defensive of your actions; just live your life according to the Word. Defend those who cannot defend themselves - those who are abused, maltreated and oppressed. But do it according to the Word. When you do, God will defend you. Be a winner.

Missions Field Testimony

It was also while we were in South Africa that the unthinkable happened. I remember clearly where I was when they brought her. It was her aunt who had carried her and ran into one of the tents we were in. I remember I was with a patient; I was the only triage nurse on duty that day. The aunt said that the little girl had been raped by her uncle, so that he could be purified and get rid of the HIV in his system. She was just two-and-a-half years.

I was in so much shock, but at the same time the mother and nurse in me went into action. I took the girl from her aunt. She was trembling. When I tried to touch her perineal area to examine her, she took my hand away forcefully. She was terrified. I tried so much to calm her down, to soothe her. It was excruciating to clean her up; there was blood and mucus everywhere. It was impossible.

We finally calmed her down, so we could examine and medicate her. A lot left me that day. I don't think I was ever the same. I tried to check on her as much as I could. I remember going back the next year. I bought clothes and toys but we couldn't locate her. I don't know what happened to her - if she ever got tested and what the results were. I can only pray that she's okay.

Today's Prayer

Lord, there's so much pain in the world; but you alone can soothe the pain and take it away. Please, comfort us. Help those that are lost to find their way so they won't hurt other people. Amen.

Further Bible Reading: Psalms 90 and 127.

Day 6

BE A RECONCILER

Bible Reading

"And all of this is a gift from God, who brought us back to himself through Christ. And God has given us this task of reconciling people to him. For God was in Christ, reconciling the world to himself, no longer counting people's sins against them. And he gave us this wonderful message of reconciliation." —2 Corinthians 5:18-19

Winning Thought

Soul-winners are ultimate winners! Winners hunger to follow God's heart by loving people and reconciling them back to Christ. As winners, we are called to the ministry of reconciliation. When you win a soul, you become wiser and you keep winning!

Mission Field Testimony

We arrived in Kenya with a passion to win souls for Christ. It was my second visit. We were visiting the Kibera Slums, one of the largest slums in the world. The medical mission was for three days. By the end of the first day, we had seen over 900 patients. The queue was so long. I remember seeing people with desperation on their faces. We cared for them and gave our best to them.

At one point, we were cleaning a wound on a lady's leg and it had taken about two hours. We didn't know that a nurse practitioner had been watching us from afar. She was a Muslim; her face and head were covered in hijab. She walked up to where we were and asked, "Why do you care so much for these people?" She wanted to know the reason we came. I told her that Christ had sent us and He was our inspiration for loving the people. After a long conversation, she accepted Jesus into her heart as her Savior.

It was one of the happiest days of my life. To know that someone can see the LOVE of God and be transformed by it.

When a soul is won to God's Kingdom, there is a great rejoicing. That gives me strength and keeps me winning.

Today's Prayer

Lord, please, use me in any way you can to bring people back to you. I want to be a reconciler of people. And if I have caused any division or stumbling, please help me to change and make amends. Let me never get tired of winning souls for you. Amen.

Further Bible Reading: James 1 and 2.

DAY 7

ENOUGH IS ENOUGH

Bible Reading

"No power in the sky above or in the earth below—indeed, nothing in all creation will ever be able to separate us from the love of God that is revealed in Christ Jesus our Lord." —Romans 8:39

Winning Thought

We have heard over and over again, winners don't quit and quitters don't win. Well, there are things in life we must quit to win. Quit hating, quit grudging, quit the accusations, quit gossiping, quit the blame game, quit the unhealthy competition and comparison

Enough is enough! I think I love this phrase so much. Winners can come to the point of saying enough is enough. Praise God! What's holding you back? Tell that thing or person, enough is enough!

Mission Field Testimony

We had gone to Nigeria on an evangelical mission at a church. There, the pastor had looked at me and decided that I was dressed like a prostitute because I had lipstick and nail polish. I was told to take the polish off before I could minister. By the grace of God and the power of the Holy Spirit leading, I obeyed the Pastor and using my teeth, I removed the nail polish from my nails. I actually cut one of my fingers doing that and had to cover it with a bandaid. I proceeded to remove the lipstick and my makeup from my face.

Once I was called to minister, I took one look at the church and saw sadness, hopelessness, depression and all kinds of weariness. The spirit of heaviness took over my body, and my mind. I could feel the pain of these people and I had never met them before. The Spirit of God opened my mouth and the words "enough is enough" poured out. I repeated it over and over, and the whole church started chanting those words back.

We started dancing and clapping and shouting and raising our voices in praises to God. It was a wondrous sight to behold. Those worn-out, downtrodden people suddenly were dancing and rejoicing, delivered and set free from every bondage holding them down.

That day, the tide turned for good in that church, and by the end of that service, the Pastor was dancing and singing. I remember the son of the pastor started crying and when we asked him why, he said he had never seen his father dance before or sing with joy. God delivered that church that day.

Enough is enough! We need to quit the negativity and embrace the love of God. If I had not obeyed the Holy Spirit, I don't know what would've happened to the church. Oh, by the way, the Pastor and I became good friends and he has been a blessing to my ministry.

Today's Prayer

Lord, deliver me from judging others and help me to respond with love all the time because love does cover a multitude of sins. When my brother or sister wrongs me, help me to cover them with your love. I love you, Lord. Amen.

Further Bible Reading: John 14 and 15.

Day 8

THE TRIUMPH OF FAITH

Bible Reading

"Faith shows the reality of what we hope for; it is the evidence of things we cannot see. Through their faith, the people in days of old earned a good reputation."
—*Hebrews 11:1-2*

Winning Thought

To win in life, we must first be willing to put our foot in the water. Sometimes, that's the wakeup call we need to embark on a life-transforming journey. The water may be cold, dirty, deep, uncertain - but just put your foot in; just do it!

Winners have an everlasting love story. People say, "Lord, change my story." No, I don't want the Lord to change my story. My story has been written long before time. It's a beautiful story covered by the blood of Jesus. It's a victorious story, it's a heavenly story, it's a love story. I just need to walk into and live my story.

Mission Field Testimony

I had met this amazing lady, who invited me to her country, Suriname. I had never heard of this place before. When the plan for Suriname Medical Missions were finalized, we were so excited, all bags packed. The next day, we got news that plans had changed and our hosts were no longer willing to host us.

I remember Dr. Wole saying we would still go and that God would provide us a help. Unfortunately, I couldn't go the same day the whole team left due to work-related issues. I landed in Paramaribo a day after everyone else, alone and no direction of where I was going. I remember being put in a taxi and setting out to a land in which I had no clue of what was ahead. I sat in that taxi and thought of all kinds of things that could go wrong. I could get raped and killed and no one would know what had happened to me. There was no phone communication to let the others know where I was. All I had was the name of a Pastor and the name of a village.

In that taxi that day, I made up my mind that I would get to my destination. I changed my thoughts to godly, faith-filled thoughts. I refused to let fear rule over me. Well, I did get to my destination. I met my team and a church was planted by the end of our trip and many souls were saved. If not for God, if not for the Holy Spirit, if not for His grace and mercy, I might have been discouraged.

You must be willing to put your foot in the water, God will do the rest.

Today's Prayer

Who is like my Rock? Who is like God? No one can do the things you do. You are a shield around me, the glory and the lifter of my head. You have set me apart to accomplish your plans. Thank you for trusting me to do that. Amen.

Further Bible Reading: Psalms 23, 24 and 25.

DAY 9

MAKE BETTER PLANS

Bible Reading

"Commit your actions to the Lord, and your plans will succeed." —Proverbs 16:3

Winning Thoughts

Winners plan. Have a vision of where you are going. Take responsibility for the outcome of your life. Winners ask questions: Where am I going? What am I doing? Asking yourself these questions will help you gain clarity of purpose. For instance, are you claiming to have a business but have no goals? Learn from the architect. Envision your target from the beginning. Then, start drawing; start building the end-product before the earnings. Yes, winners plan!

Mission Field Testimony

We had gone to Belize in December 2018 for the

JustDoIt women's conference. During the meeting, the Lord spoke to me to assist one woman in starting a small business. She was an immigrant who had come to support her daughter that had a new baby. She had left her business with no hope of maintaining it while away in a foreign land. As I would later learn, she had prayed to God to provide her with the funds she would use to resuscitate her business once she got back to her country. I was specifically instructed to provide part of the capital for her. I thought I would be able to do it from my savings, but I ran out of funds, due to so many unexpected expenditures (I apparently hadn't planned well).

Meanwhile, the conference had been an extraordinary one and the women had been inspired to believe that they could never suffer or lose with God. I believed there had to be a way out. Thankfully, at that meeting, an offering was raised to meet the needs of that immigrant woman. Indeed, God heard her prayers and, that day, she got more than enough to start her business. God is faithful; He will not allow you to suffer. You must win!

Today's Prayer

Lord, supply all the resources I need to move ahead in my business. Send the men and women you have set aside to help me progress in life. Let me meet my destiny accelerators quickly and let them work for my good. I trust you, Lord. Amen

Further Bible Reading: Matthew 4, 5.

DAY 10

FIGHT FOR YOUR LIFE AND SUFFER NO MORE

Bible Reading

"Just then a woman who had suffered for twelve years with constant bleeding came up behind him. She touched the fringe of his robe, for she thought, "If I can just touch his robe, I will be healed." Jesus turned around, and when he saw her he said, "Daughter, be encouraged! Your faith has made you well." And the woman was healed at that moment." —Matthew 9:20-22

Winning Thought

Winners decide not to suffer anymore. What is causing stress? Let it go. If you need to spend more time at home and rest more, then do it. Yes, you can take off a couple of days and just relax. I do it, even if it means shutting off people and conversations. Turn off that phone. Are you constantly worried?

Do meditations on God's Word, sing songs and dance. Are you sick? Sometimes healthy eating and rest do wonders. Are you suffering from financial stress due to high bills? Find ways to reduce bills by planning better and budgeting. Winners understand that managing wealth successfully exalts God.

Mission Field Testimony

While in Tanzania, we visited a rural area with predominantly poor and less-privileged people. There were so many people who needed assistance; you could see it in their eyes and posture. They just didn't want to hear well-prepared speeches or sermons. They were hungry. As we served them, we sang songs of praise and ministered to them in prayers.

The presence of God was mighty at the gathering - so much that a lady jumped up, running around the church. She later testified that she had sickle cell disease and had often been in so much pain; but as she came in to the church and joined in the dancing, the pain left her body.

Winners decide that the time to suffer is limited. You let go of what brings stress and walk on the pathway of healing.

Today's Prayer

Lord, just like you removed suffering and distress from the life of the woman with the issue of blood, please remove suffering from my life. Help me to understand that the power to walk in good health is in my hands. Thank you, Lord. Amen

Further Bible Reading: Psalms 1 and 2.

DAY 11

HOPE IN DESPERATE TIMES

Bible Reading

"Here is another illustration Jesus used: "The Kingdom of Heaven is like a mustard seed planted in a field. It is the smallest of all seeds, but it becomes the largest of garden plants; it grows into a tree, and birds come and make nests in its branches." —Matthew 13:31-32

Winning Thought

Winners are not interested in building PRIVATE kingdoms. Winners build communities. Winners build people to become winners. They give of themselves, while protecting their integrity and their salvation. Winners are kingdom builders.

Mission Field Testimony

It was in the wake of a tsunami in Japan. I met people desperate to know the true God. We had planned to go for a gospel concert tour, but the journey turned into a missionary trip. It was difficult to go on this trip. There were fears of radiation killing people. The plane we flew on was empty, just a few going to Japan. But I made up my mind to go to Japan to sing about Jesus. I knew there was HOPE, and HOPE makes the heart strong again.

The tsunami had killed so many and left many more desolate. We shared the good news we brought and the love of God. Many got saved and many we delivered. Multitudes were restored to a new life, even at the cost of our comfort, sanity and freedom. I was sick throughout the trip. Indeed, but for God, I would have died.

Still, it proved to be a worthwhile trip because I witnessed the miracles that God did in the lives of so many people. We didn't go there to build our private kingdoms; we helped build communities that will last forever.

Today's Prayer

Lord, I want to be a kingdom builder. I don't want to build my own private world that will collapse. If you don't build with me, my work will not be done well. I want to work with you to give hope to others. Amen.

Further Bible Reading: Psalms 3 and 4.

Day 12

SUCCESS TAKES HARD WORK!

Bible Reading

"Dear brothers and sisters, if another believer is overcome by some sin, you who are godly should gently and humbly help that person back onto the right path. And be careful not to fall into the same temptation yourself. Share each other's burdens, and in this way obey the law of Christ. If you think you are too important to help someone, you are only fooling yourself. You are not that important. Pay careful attention to your own work, for then you will get the satisfaction of a job well done, and you won't need to compare yourself to anyone else. For we are each responsible for our own conduct." —Galatians 6:1-5

Winning Thought

Winners are facilitators of other people's breakthroughs. They place themselves in the position to help others achieve success. Winners know that they are solutions to problems. They know they are the hands and feet of God in the world and they surrender themselves, willingly.

Mission Field Testimony

It was my first time in Rwanda. There, I met a young man - actually, he wasn't that young, but he looked like a teenager. Our lodging had been in a nun's home. It was like a B&B; we were served breakfast every morning. The young man helped us in bringing foods, getting hot water, cleaning up the dining area, and the likes. He would follow me around and called me "mom". People teased me that I had a "big son" and that I should adopt him.

At one point, I took the suggestion very serious. I adopted the young man, in my heart. I promised to care for him and support his education. We got him a laptop, paid his school fees and helped him start a small business. Most importantly, we reconnected him to God, and established him in a local church.

It's been 8 years since then, and the young man has graduated from college and currently pursuing his graduate degrees. He's thriving, living on his own, trying to make it work. He will be successful because the foundation has been laid. He is winning!

Today's Prayer

Lord, I want to help others succeed. I want to care for others the way you do. Let your love fill up all the spaces in my heart. Holy Spirit, my Caregiver, show me the pathway to care for others. Amen.

Further Bible Reading: Psalms 6 and 7.

Day 13

FORGET YOUR HATERS

Bible Reading

"Praise the Lord, who is my rock. He trains my hands for war and gives my fingers skill for battle. He is my loving ally and my fortress, my tower of safety, my rescuer. He is my shield, and I take refuge in him. He makes the nations submit to me." —Psalm 144:1-2

Winning Thought

Winners understand that they don't have to fit in with those around them. They know that they can be looked upon as strange individuals. Winners know that their values and lifestyles might seem a little different from the rest of the world. But it's okay to be you! Your focus always should be: "I'm on the pathway to victory; JESUS is leading the way."

Forget the people who won't accept you. Forge ahead. God is your Ally. You are a winner, and certainly, a winner you shall be!

Mission Field Testimony

We had gone to Suriname that first time and it was a difficult journey - a journey made more difficult by the fact that we did not know where we were going to stay and who would come to our medical station. We were told to go to a nearby village and ask the king of the village to allow us set up in their village square. The king refused, stating that we were Christians and he didn't want anyone bringing religion to his village. We were disappointed and felt the rejection.

Our interpreter took us to another village. At first, we were reluctant to go. We could have gone back home but we knew God is our Ally; He leads the way. When we arrived at that new village, they accepted us with so much joy. They told us that they had been praying for us to come for days. We lifted up the name of Jesus in that place and God did miracles there. So many people got saved. Hundreds got healed and delivered, despite the fact that someone else had rejected us and God's message.

People may reject you but God will help you forge forward. He will bring people who will accept you.

Today's Prayer

Lord, protect me from feeling down when I get rejected. Help me see that You are working everything out for my good. Bring people that will assist me and work with me to become successful. I decree and declare that I have favor everywhere I go, in your sight and in the sight of men. Amen.

Further Bible Reading: John 14 and 15.

Day 14

POWER OF SEPARATION

Bible Reading

"Put on all of God's armor so that you will be able to stand firm against all strategies of the devil. For we are not fighting against flesh-and-blood enemies, but against evil rulers and authorities of the unseen world, against mighty powers in this dark world, and against evil spirits in the heavenly places." —Ephesians 6:11-12

Winning Thought

Winners know that God trains us during hard times. We know that when attacks come, our sure anchor and succor is God's WORD. Winners know that these trials and tribulations we face can NEVER overcome us because the WINNING KING reigns in our lives. We understand that separation is not necessarily bad.

To become a winner, you must learn the power of separation. To separate good and evil, your enemies and friends, your future and your past, your family and distractions, your dream-boosters and dream-killers, your destiny helpers and destiny destroyers. I can go on.

Choose whom you will follow, and do it right. Separate and deal wisely. You will definitely succeed. Let's keep winning! Nothing can stop us now. Our victory is perfected. Yes, we are winners.

Come on, say it loudly to yourself: "I am winning!"

Mission Field Testimony

I have always desired to have lots of money, so I can help a lot of people. When you meet people, you must make a decision to see the good and not the bad. But when you do see the bad, choose Christ in resolving issues.

We meet all kinds of people during our mission trips. Some can push you to the limits, while others are so sweet and unforgettable. I still remember Wagner, the little boy from one of the favelas in Brazil. He had been born to a teenage mother who was only 13 years-old. She had left him with his grandmother to pursue a better life with older men.

As at the time of our arrival, Wagner had lost his

grandmother and was now living in the favela, scouting for food and a place to sleep. One of our hosts had accommodated him in his home and that was where I met him. We cooked food for all the kids living in the favela and thereafter shared stories. As we got ready to leave, Wagner clung to me and refused to let go, until after much persuasion.

I don't know where Wagner is now. He must have grown into a young man. I still pray for him and hope I can see him again.

Today's Prayer

Lord, protect the children who have no parents and those who are lost. Be a shield around them. Provide parents for them who will really take care of their needs. Keep them safe forever. Amen

Further Bible Reading: Matthew 7 and 8.

Day 15

WINNERS ARE GIVERS

Bible Reading

"Then he said to the crowd, "If any of you wants to be my follower, you must give up your own way, take up your cross daily, and follow me. If you try to hang on to your life, you will lose it. But if you give up your life for my sake, you will save it." —Luke 9:23-24

Winning Thought

Winners are givers. They give everything. I mean EVERYTHING - your life, your time, your money, your pleasure, your suffering, your knowledge, your ambitions, your plans...everything!

Mission Field Testimony

It was another beautiful day in China. We had prayed that morning and decided to go to the market to tell people about the good news we had brought. We had interacted with so many people and all was going so well. We were filled with joy.

All of a sudden, we saw police everywhere coming towards our direction. I remember that my heart sank and fear gripped me. I turned around and I saw a way to escape. They won't see me if I run now, I had told myself. However, at that moment, I remembered Luke 9:23-24. "…If you try to hang on to your life, you will lose it…" For the second time that week, I surrendered to God. Even though we were rounded up and interrogated, they allowed us to leave. Glory to God. We had heard of horrible things that happened to others but God preserved us that day.

As Christians, we must be ready to take up the cross and follow Jesus. After we left there, we went to another area. We continued to minister to the people we met by the roadside. Before the end of that trip, we had seen many give their lives to Christ.

Today's Prayer

Lord, the protection you give is the best. You will always protect us from danger and fear. Drive evil away from us and may we live under your guidance. Amen.

Further Bible Reading: Matthew 11 and 12.

Day 16

THE GREAT EXCHANGE

Bible Reading

"Don't worry about anything; instead, pray about everything. Tell God what you need, and thank him for all he has done. Then you will experience God's peace, which exceeds anything we can understand. His peace will guard your hearts and minds as you live in Christ Jesus." —Philippians 4:6-7

Winning Thought

Winners trade by barter! Yes, it's an old adage. To trade by barter means you have something in your hands and you want to exchange it for something you want or need. You can't be a hoarder and win. There won't be space for progress. Exchange that unforgiveness and bitterness for peace and joy. Share the business ideas you have; you might get one back that can help boost your business or ministry.

Exchange things you don't need for things that you desperately need. Sometimes, you have to bring something to the table!

Mission Field Testimony

When we were in Johannesburg, South Africa, we met a pregnant woman, who had high blood pressure. It was so high she was in danger of having complications with her pregnancy. She was so scared and very lonely. Her husband was not there and so many people had wronged her. She was carrying so much burden, you could feel the weight of it on her shoulder. She didn't realize that she was killing herself and her unborn child because of this excess baggage she carried. She had unforgiveness and bitterness, malice and so much sadness.

The doctor explained that the medications we had were not strong enough to bring her blood pressure down but we still cared for her and prayed along with her. When she poured her heart out to us, we encouraged her to let go of all the anger and bitterness and let God heal her from inside out. She agreed. She took the medication, ate and just sat with us for a long while. She was able to relax and enjoy seeing all the work God was doing in others. We saw her laugh at our stories and later when I rechecked her pressure it was down significantly. Glory to God!

She was given instructions on relaxation techniques and told to continue to monitor her pressure. She was told to follow up with her physician and learn to live in freedom from negative thoughts.

What are you holding on to? It may be the cause of your illness or restlessness. God wants you to exchange the baggage of hatred, unforgiveness and bitterness with the fruits of the Spirit. Learn to let go because the price is eternal life forever.

Today's Prayer

Lord, so many have hurt and harmed me. You saw them, you know them but I will give this pain and sorrow and anger to you. Take it from me and give me the fruit of the Spirit, in Jesus' name Amen.

Further Bible Reading: Proverbs 30 and 31.

Day 17

CHOOSE WISDOM

Bible Reading

"Using a dull ax requires great strength, so sharpen the blade. That's the value of wisdom; it helps you succeed." —Ecclesiastes 10:10

Winning Thought

Winners, get wisdom. A powerful and necessary ingredient to winning – indeed, my recommendation for being wise – is being immersed in the books of Proverbs and Psalms. Every year, I read the entirety of both books. They speak to the heart and compel you to act wisely.

As you are winning, remember that winners are flexible and accommodating, but not to the detriment of their visions and pathway to victory. Winners write their visions down. When you write your vision down, it triples the power. That's what makes you a wise winner!

Mission Field Testimony

It was after Hurricane Katrina that I decided to be a missionary. I didn't even know that there was something called "medical missions". I am so glad to have met Dr. Wole, who showed me what a true medical servant is.

That year, I had written down my visions and prayed over them. I asked God to provide the resources that I needed to go on missions. Most times, I don't have the funds to sponsor my mission trips; but God often uses other people, hospitals and organizations to assist me. It has been a humbling position to be in, knowing that I do have and make a lot of money. Sometimes I put my needs and the needs of my extended family aside because there are sick people that God wants to use my hands and feet to heal.

To be able to go and serve as a nurse and help those in need has brought me so much satisfaction and peace of mind. It is therapeutic for me and I hope that people will understand that. I will choose going on mission trips a thousand times over and I'm grateful that I get to do what I love. Helping others, whether they are my family or strangers, always gives me the greatest joy.

Today's Prayer

Lord, do not let me stop this hunger to serve you and others. Help me not pass by and watch the poor suffer. In all I can give, may I give my very best. Amen.

Further Bible Reading: Psalms 18 and 19.

Day 18

THE PEACEMAKERS

Bible Reading

"God blesses those who work for peace, for they will be called the children of God." —Matthew 5:9

Winning Thought

"God blesses those who work for peace…" Wow, I love it. Winners must be peacemakers. Pursuing peace leads to a victorious life. It leads to a healthy life. The process itself can be tiring, exhausting and humiliating at times, but the end result of having made peace is…priceless!

Mission Field Testimony

I met him, the village drunk. Everyone knew him. They talked about him. They avoided him on the roadside. This was in Guyana. When I started talking to him, you could smell the alcohol on his breath. He was not clean; you could see he hadn't showered for days.

At first, he was resistant and a little aggressive but before long he became excited that someone was talking to him, especially a foreigner. He started telling me about his children that lived in New York. How he hadn't seen them for years; they didn't want anything to do with him. He was so sad about that, he started crying. All he wanted, he said, was for him to unite with them again. I asked him if he could let Jesus help him? He agreed and, right there, prayed with me to accept Jesus into his life.

After getting saved, he was quiet and you could tell by looking at his face that he had peace. He had only one request: "Can you call my children and tell them that I am saved and changed?" I told him I would do that, as soon I got back to the United States. He brought out a rumpled, dirty piece of paper from his pocket which contained the phone numbers of his children - you could tell he'd been carrying it around with him. His children were dear to his heart but he couldn't reach them.

Once I got home I called his children and told them what had happened to their father. They were happy that someone had seen their dad and that he was well.

God has called us to be peacemakers. Will you extend a hand of peace? Keep winning!

Today's Prayer

Lord, your exceeding great love amazes me, so I will praise you. Help me to realize that you see the depths of my heart and you love me anyway. Thank you, for your acts of kindness towards me. Amen.

Further Bible Reading: Psalm 27.

Day 19

SPILLS HAPPEN, CLEAN IT UP

Bible Reading

"I will send you the seasonal rains. The land will then yield its crops, and the trees of the field will produce their fruit." —*Leviticus 26:4*

Winning Thought

You know how you are told, "If it spills, clean it"? Well, I say, if it spills, look at the spill and see what spilled, make an estimate - how much will it cost to fix it - before you start cleaning. It will help prevent making future mistakes (spillage control) because most times we start cleaning too early and end up spilling again.

Mission Field Testimony

She was a single mother and she had no one. She was strong, resilient and a lover of Christ. She pastored a church and was very influential in her community. I remember clearly the first time I saw her; she reminded me of the Biblical Naomi. She loved God but she was in pain. Her church was in danger of collapsing and she had young children to feed and care for. She had the villagers looking up to her for guidance, when she herself was in pain.

I wanted to teach the young adults in my church how to give back, so I took them to Belize. We had visited the church and saw, firsthand, the damage; the roof was leaking and people were sitting on the floor. We wanted to fix the roof but, upon assessment, we found out that the church had no foundation.

I had no money to commence such a project but I have a God who can do the Impossible. After talking with my Pastors and my family, we started a fundraiser. Together, with RCCGNA Young Adults, we rebuilt the church, from the ground up. It took us ten days to make building materials and initiate the construction. It was a beautiful transformation. We gave this woman of God a chance to watch her church grow and to start a new life in her community.

The task may seem too much, but God is able to finish anything He commits into your hands to do. He is faithful and reliable. The church was broken but after a good estimate was made, it was restored again to being a beautiful place

Today's Prayer

Consider my heart, Lord. Please work on it and help my unbelief. When things seem impossible, give me the faith to believe in your miracles again. Thank you. Amen.

Further Bible Reading: Luke 11 and 12.

Day 20
FINDING YOUR WAY

Bible Reading

"The warden had no more worries, because Joseph took care of everything. The Lord was with him and caused everything he did to succeed." —Genesis 39:23

Winning Thought

Winners don't wait for someone to turn their light on. They invent the light. In fact, they are the light! I once heard an actor say, "I'm not worried, I'm just winning!" It's amazing how we as Christians worry over things we can't do much about. How you doing? Remember those favorite words from TV personality, Wendy? Well, get an attitude, as you look in the mirror and ask yourself "How you doing?" Answer with a big, "Yes, yes, yes, I'm doing fabulous!" Stop worrying, the battle is won already. Look at yourself and say, "I'm winning!"

Mission Field Testimony

We once got lost in Rwanda. (I have to laugh, telling this story. We do have lots of funny things happen on the mission field. Thank God, who causes us to laugh at things that could have gone the other way!) That first trip to Rwanda was filled with testimonies. We met this lady; she was a passionate "Christian" and she convinced us to go with her to eat "Nigerian food" at a restaurant, near where we stayed. She said, "It's just around the corner; we can walk."

We started out with her and the short journey turned into a long one. First, she talked us into taking a taxi, after we got tired of walking. Then we got off and started walking again. "It's right there!" she kept saying, but we never saw the place. It had grown dark outside and by this time we were scared. We talked amongst ourselves that we should go back home but we still followed her like "mumus".

Finally, we got to the restaurant and it was empty and shabby. We couldn't even eat there, and almost at once, we decided that this was not a safe place to be and we needed to leave. The struggle to get home began and by now we were so scared. The lady had abandoned us and refused to help us get home. Oh, we prayed and prayed.

We finally found a small car and all of us managed to squeeze inside the car to go home. I remember one of us started doing a video with his phone, in case we were never found, so that someone would know what had happened to us. God spared us that day and everyday afterwards.

Today's Prayer

Lord, I am forever grateful that you are not a God that abandons people, even when we deserve it. You still rescue us and keep us safe. Thank you. Amen.

Further Bible Reading: Revelation 2, 3 and 4.

Day 21

PURSUE WHAT MATTERS

Bible Reading

"Seek the Kingdom of God above all else, and he will give you everything you need." —Luke 12:31

Winning Thought

Winners are Kings! Kings pursue the things of the Kingdom. When you do, you will remain a winner forever. God reigns in their lives! But Paupers pursue things of the world. Worldly kingdom will not bring lasting peace. Pursue the right things that matter and have eternal benefits.

Missions Field Testimony

It was supposed to be an ordinary trip. I had planned everything. This was one mission that I was one of the lead facilitators. It was to be in my state of origin. Again, due to my hectic work schedule, my team went ahead of me. My flight was to take me to a city closer to where the mission would be. This was my first time of taking that route to Enugu.

As we approached landing, the unthinkable happened; a plane had crashed-landed ahead of us. It was a small plane and had left debris on the runway. So we were told that we couldn't land. For the next several hours, we tried to find an airport to land but none would allow us. Finally we landed in Lagos, another city and was told that we needed to wait for clearance before we could complete our journey.

We stayed in Lagos for two days and I was missing out on the mission trip that I had gone for. Everyone said, "Go home. Maybe God didn't want you to come to this trip." But I knew the covenant I had made with God - all missions must be completed once initiated by God. I decided to board a vehicle to my destination and, despite the hazards, was able to make it on time for just one more day left out of the missions. I saw people and ministered to them. My heart was full even if I could serve for just a couple of minutes.

Kings pursue the Kingdom. I choose to see that whatever I do for God matters. It's not the quantity but the quality; it's my heart of service that matters, not the length of service. I went back home, feeling accomplished and God did His part of getting me home safely.

Today's Prayer

Your instructions are clear, Lord: "Love the Lord with all your heart." Please, teach me to love you with all my heart and all my strength and all my might, in Jesus' name. Amen.

Further Bible Reading: Deuteronomy 33 and 34.

Day 22

LOVE IN ACTION

Bible Reading

"Jesus replied, "'You must love the Lord your God with all your heart, all your soul, and all your mind."
—Matthew 22:37

Winning Thought

Winners know that love is not just a verbal expression. Worldly love is loud and unstable but God's love is an unending cycle of actions to prove it. Winners that love like this are in vogue.

Winners are content but they never stall in the quest for success. They believe in inventions. They know that the quest for wisdom and knowledge continues and they continue working towards being the best they can be. When they find this contentment, they show it by pouring out God's love to themselves and to others

Mission Field Testimonies

My husband and I have always been missionaries, even before I officially joined medical missions. We had a ministry called LOVE IN ACTION. We believe that words of love are not enough to show people that God cares; we must demonstrate it by our actions. Our ministry fed widows, paid school fees for underprivileged children, and paid hospital bills for the poor and the sick.

One time, we had gone home on a visit and I met this woman, who was a first time mother with a newborn baby. I watched her trying to breastfeed the baby but he kept on crying and was so fussy. You could see that he was very hungry and frustrated that he was not getting enough food. I then saw the mom bring "pap" and was trying to feed the newborn. I screamed, "No, he's too young to eat solids." But she told me that since she was not eating well, she couldn't make enough breast milk for her baby and she wanted to force feed him with the pap.

I remember crying that day as I took the baby from her. We went and bought baby milk and food for her. When I got back to the US, I bought baby food and lots of other things and sent them to her.

It has been a rewarding journey working for the Lord and I will do it again and again. It really doesn't cost much; you just need to be faithful and obedient. Once you love God and yourself, you can love another. This love must begin inside of you; it cannot be wished on or forced on.

Today's Prayer

When I am weak in showing love, Lord, make me strong. Let me never give up in showing Agape love - the love you show to humanity. Forgive me for the times I have not loved myself. Holy Spirit, teach me to love you, love me and love others. Amen.

Further Bible Reading: 1 Corinthians 13, 14 and 15.

Day 23

THE HEART OF A KING

Bible Reading

"But the Lord said to Joshua, "I have given you Jericho, its king, and all its strong warriors." —Joshua 6:2

Winning Thought

Winners honor their leaders and are respectful of authority. Winners repent easily without looking for justifications. They allow themselves to be corrected!

Winners do not emerge by democratic election. They emerge by divine appointments. God appoints us winners; it's not by the votes of people. Hallelujah! Come on, let's win!

Mission Field Testimony

Suriname will always be a wonder to me. God did so many testimonies there. We had been kicked out of one village and we finally found a place to minister to people. We were having church when someone came and told our interpreter that the king in that village was sick. We went to pray for him, and once we arrived, we met some group of women who told us that they too had been praying for God to send help to their village. They told us that they had specifically prayed for people to come from America. They didn't know how God would do it but that was what they desired. They said they had told God that if He brought people from America, it would prove to them that He exists.

Incidentally, we had almost terminated our planned visit to Suriname because our host had cancelled at the last minute. But God is not like man, He keeps His word. He had promised these women that help would come, and there we were, sent by God. We prayed for the king and he instantly got healed. He had been diagnosed with congenital heart failure and had been so swollen, weak and bedridden. But he got up and was able to speak to us.

There was a great joy in that village that day. Multitudes, including the king, gave their lives to Christ. Glory to God.

Don't let anything distract you from God's plan and purpose for your life.

Today's Prayer

Lord, I will go wherever you send me. I will bear witness to your great name. I will be your ambassador. Help me Lord, not to turn back. May I have the courage not to give up, even when things look difficult. Amen.

Further Bible Reading: Daniel 1, 2 and 3.

Day 24

FOLLOW THE INSTRUCTIONS

Bible Reading

"Dear woman, that's not our problem," Jesus replied. "My time has not yet come." But his mother told the servants, "Do whatever he tells you." Standing nearby were six stone water jars, used for Jewish ceremonial washing. Each could hold twenty to thirty gallons."
—John 2:4-6

Winning Thought

Winners follow INSTRUCTIONS. As one of my favorite preachers of the Word, Jeremiah Asomugha, always says, "The miracles are in the instruction". Winners understand the instruction Mary said to the disciples, "Do whatever he tells you." Winners JUST DO IT! Hah!

Mission Field Testimony

We had been in Kathmandu, Nepal, for a while. We knew all the people who served us in the place we were staying. One of them was a young man, named Anu. I can't forget this miracle. It was astounding. He had come to fix the window unit that was not cooling and while doing his work, the man of God had asked him if he was saved. He said no. The moment he spoke, we knew something was wrong with the way he sounded. His tongue was curled and he was almost dumb but not completely.

He started telling us about all kinds of gods he served - thousands of small gods. He had prayed to them to heal him so he could speak well and make progress with his life. He said that he often gave the gods food and anything else they wanted. And yet he was not healed.

So, the man of God said, "Why has none of these gods healed you?" He said maybe he needed to give them more things. The man of God then told Anu about a God who needs nothing from us but to have faith and that if he had faith, he would be healed. After many instructions from God's Word were given, Anu believed and was instantly healed; right in front us, he could speak well. He immediately called his brother and, as he spoke with his him, we could hear the brother on the other end screaming with joy. Anu told him how he got saved and how God healed him.

What a miracle! Not only was Anu healed physically but his soul was delivered from eternal destruction. He and his family were all saved. He is still healed today. Glory to God!

Today's Prayer

Oh Lord, You can do miracles. Thank you for healing ...(insert a name). We give you all the glory and honor, and we will continue to praise you forever. Amen.

Further Bible Reading: Mark 1 and 2.

Day 25

THE POWERFUL WORD

Bible Reading

"In the beginning the Word already existed. The Word was with God, and the Word was God. He existed in the beginning with God. God created everything through him, and nothing was created except through him. The Word gave life to everything that was created, and his life brought light to everyone." —John 1:1-4

Winning Thought

Winners understand they are chosen and called to do mighty things. They hear the Word of God. They are in tune with the one who is the WORD. And who sent the word! Winners understand that everything God does, He does with words. Winners know that they can't be other people. Winners can only be themselves, because other people are already taken.

Mission Field Testimonies

I will still continue to testify about this beautiful nation of Suriname. We had almost concluded our mission work on this particular visit. The trip was a scary one too because we literally stayed by a gold coast and there weren't many amenities. That was the day I had to clean up with the precious last bottle of drinking water I had. I wasn't gonna shower with water filled with gold fillings.

We had finished and were packing to go home but this group of women came with this lady in a wheelbarrow. She was very sick; she had the Chikungunya virus. There was nothing much we could do, except to give her all the medicine and pray over her. As one of our Pastors prayed, he asked God to heal the woman while we were still present in the village because the friends expected her to be well. While we believed in our hearts by faith that she was healed, we didn't see the physical manifestation. We were a little down, but the man of God that prayed kept believing.

We packed up and got into our van and drove off. I still remember what happened next, as if it were yesterday. As our van drove off, it wasn't long after we heard shouting and screaming. We looked through the back window of the van and saw them running after our van, hands flailing in the air, beckoning us to stop. We stopped and literally thought that the lady had died. We were so apprehensive. As they reached our van, they proclaimed, "She's healed. She's healed. She got up. She's eating. She's Okay." Glory to God!

What a gift God gave us that day! What joy! What a miracle! The Word of God never fails. The word is powerful and can do wonders.

Today's Prayer

Lord, I speak your powerful word over everyone that is in trouble right now. I speak that they are delivered and they are free. Lord, I pray that no weapon formed against them can ever prosper. Lord, I pray that every sickness is healed in Jesus' name. Amen.

Further Bible Reading: Psalm 119.

Day 26

BROKEN PIECES

Bible Reading

"Jesus took the five loaves and two fish, looked up toward heaven, and blessed them. Then, breaking the loaves into pieces, he kept giving the bread and fish to the disciples so they could distribute it to the people."
—Luke 9:16

Winning Thought

Winners understand the principles of brokenness. Jesus blessed the loaves, broke them into pieces and gave them to the disciples to give to the people. The loaves kept multiplying. Sometimes we must be broken in order to multiply. Winners present themselves to Jesus to be broken, not to man. Man's brokenness is torture, but God's brokenness is victory. Are you ready to be broken and blessed - to be a winner? Let's win!

Mission Field Testimony

The women in the slums of Kibera in Nairobi Kenya had been neglected and uncared for. They mostly had no shoes on; they came barefooted. They carried their babies on their backs and some had not showered for days.

As we cared for them, I could see their feet and hands had been so broken, so dry and cracked. As a woman, my heart bled for them. Once I got back to the States, God imprinted in my heart to buy things to wash their feet and hands and to do pedicure and paint them with nice nail polish.

The Holy Ghost and I have a very serious and peculiar relationship. When He tells me to do something, I don't argue; I just do it. So, I prepared for that trip and got everything ready. Once we arrived back to the slums, I invited the women and they all came. That day, there were so many. I washed their feet and cleaned them and painted them. The women and I cried so much that day and it was refreshing soul-washing tears.

My friends and team members came and joined me. We all washed the feet of these women. The Holy Spirit spoke to me that day with my head bent down washing a foot. He said, "As you washed these feet, I will wash your sins away and wash away every accusation of men.' I will acquit you of any shame and disgrace." A life-transforming day that I can never forget.

My daughter, Cherish, had seen what happened that day. I remember her crying and hugging me and thanking me for being her mommy. She told me how proud she is of me, and that made my day. To God be all the glory.

Today's Prayer

Lord, the assurance of your word; the blessings you give to us daily, are not just for us but for the whole world. Lord, teach me to fight for those who can't fight for themselves and to trust that you alone will give the victory. Help me humble myself in your mighty hands because you will exalt me. Amen.

Further Bible Reading: Proverbs 18 and 19.

DAY 27

THE POWER IN A NOSE RING

Bible Reading

"So if you sinful people know how to give good gifts to your children, how much more will your heavenly Father give the Holy Spirit to those who ask him."
—Luke 11:13

Winning Thought

Winners understand that there are three breads of idleness - gossip, self-pity and discontentment. Don't be caught in any of them this year! Continue on your pathway to victory. Embrace the components of the fruit of the Spirit - love, joy, peace, long suffering, patience and others listed in Galatians 5. You are winning!

Mission Field Testimony

I was on my last month as an intern at Lakewood Church, in Houston Texas. I made a small bet with my fellow intern. She was scared of piercing her ears; so I had gone with her to do it. I told her I would pierce my nose if she pierced her ears and she agreed. I was so scared too but I did pierce my nose that day; it was painful.

I got lots of bad attention from my family and close friends for wearing a nose ring and I really wanted to take it off. Then we got to India and I realized why I had pierced my nose. It might be irrelevant to some but it was a sign to me that God can use anything to do His work. I had met some amazing young teenage girls during our medical mission and they all clustered around me. You see, they all had nose rings. They kept pointing at my nose ring and touching theirs too. They felt a connection to me because "I looked like them." Everyone took notice and they said to me, "Stacy, this nose ring is finally doing some good!"

The girls were very sheltered and shy but they opened up to me about their fears. Some had married at the tender ages of 13 and 14. We talked about personal hygiene, menstruation and motherhood. They asked me an important question, "Can a woman be strong and beautiful too?" With joy in my heart I told them

YES! Yes! It was a #justdoit moment. I played and talked with them for hours and later showed them how to take selfies. It was easy to share Christ with them. What a powerful moment!

For every opportunity we are given, we must maximize our efforts in sharing the love of God. Sometimes, God uses foolish things to confound the wise.

Today's Prayer

Lord, use my foolishness. Turn it into your wisdom. Change my situation so that I can be brave and strong, trusting in your strength, too. Amen.

Further Bible Reading: Psalm 48 and 49.

Day 28

WATCH YOUR HEALTH

Bible Reading

"Dear friend, I hope all is well with you and that you are as healthy in body as you are strong in spirit."
—*3 John 1:2*

Winning Thought

Winners have a plan to live long. That means you must have or initiate a healthy lifestyle. Winners have no excuses for staying dormant; they pursue excellence in keeping fit. They exercise the whole body, mind and soul. It's a complete workout. No part is neglected. Are you exercising, reading books, being joyful, living in tolerance and forgiveness? Winners are not held back by anything. Come on, start your winning journey. Winners are winning. Let's win!

Mission Field Testimony

I had a difficult struggle with fibroids. It was discovered after my third pregnancy. For years, it was almost destroying my life. My blood count would get so low but never low enough to get a blood transfusion. One day, my doctor told me that the fibroids were getting bigger and I needed to remove them. I was scared because I had heard terrible stories of what could go wrong.

By God's grace, I had a successful surgery to get rid of the fibroids. At that moment, laying on the hospital bed, I made up my mind to advocate for women who are going through this horrifying ordeal.

Then I got the opportunity to travel to Nigeria with a medical team to do free surgeries on women who had fibroids. That was when I met her. Her tummy was so big and she said she had been carrying this "fake child" for so many years. She told me the story of how she had lost everything due to the fibroids - her business, her joy and her life. We shared with her that we were there to do the free surgery and that she would be a beneficiary. She was so excited and so thankful. She had the surgery and it was successful. All glory to God.

I still remember the look on her face after she woke up from the recovery room. She told me "I am finally free." We hugged and I told her, "Now, you can live again; you can start a new business and you can have children and do anything you want to." We talked about lifestyle changes and diet and staying healthy. I can't wait to see her again because I know she will have a testimony. She already has received her miracle.

Today's Prayer

Lord, everything you do is a miracle. You are the Way-maker, the Light in the darkness. Nothing is too hard for you. For everyone with fibroid issues, Lord deliver and heal them completely, in Jesus' name. Amen.

Further Bible Reading: 1 Peter 1, 2 and 3.

WINNING THOUGHTS: A 31-DAY DEVOTIONAL

Day 29

CASTING OUT DEVILS

Bible Reading

"Look, I have given you authority over all the power of the enemy, and you can walk among snakes and scorpions and crush them. Nothing will injure you."
—Luke 10:19

Winning Thought

Winners process the anointing upon them. They understand that being anointed does not mean you are appointed. You can have anointing but don't know how to control it. When you are anointed, you wait for your appointment. When appointed, you need the anointing.

With praises and worship songs, you can refresh the body, heal the mind and banish evil forces from the spirit.

Mission Field Testimony

Oh wow…I must add some more funny stories. We have encountered crazy things on the mission fields. A whole lot of crazy things and hilarious incidents have happened to us. I will share a scary but still funny one.

I had gone to Trinidad to minister in songs and do some medical mission work. My uncle who was hosting me is also a medical doctor. I had been in the church clinic downstairs, waiting to be called to minister. As I waited, someone brought a lady into the clinic. She hadn't been feeling well inside the church.

As I sat with her, I asked, "What's wrong?" She told me her tummy hurt. I could see her tummy was rounded, so I placed my right hand slightly on her tummy and started praying for her. I had just started praying and she started "demonstrating". The evil spirits were manifesting and making her shake and tremble.

If you know me, you know I don't like things like this; so I tried to leave her there but she started saying, "Help me". So, I turned back and started praying for her again. This time, I started praying in the Holy Ghost. As I prayed, my voice was getting louder and I could feel that it was straining. The devil didn't appear to be leaving soon either. My mind said, "Stacy, you will be singing soon; you want to lose your voice, casting this devil out. You don't even know how long this will take!"

I was really ready to follow my head voice and leave her but the Spirit of God told me: "You cannot leave because I have given you the authority to cast out devils." I tried arguing with God but it didn't work. So I started praying louder. The louder I prayed, the more she was demonstrating. I was getting scared now, lol. I really asked God to help me or send someone with whom I could join my faith to pray this thing out of the lady.

Finally, I saw the Pastor's wife come downstairs. She saw me with the lady and joined me to pray for her. Together, we held hands and agreed in prayer and the devil left her. She had peace and started singing songs of praise.

Indeed, if two shall agree concerning anything by faith it shall be done. Hallelujah. Thank God for sending help and for delivering that woman.

By the way, my song ministration turned out fabulous and powerful.

Today's Prayer

At the mention of the name Jesus, every knee will bow and every tongue confesses that Jesus is Lord, forever more. Thank you, Lord, that there is power in your name. Your name is a strong tower. We can run into it and be safe. Amen.

Further Bible Reading: Hebrews 11 and 12.

Day 30

A THOUSAND HALLELUJAHS

Bible Reading

"So if you sinful people know how to give good gifts to your children, how much more will your heavenly Father give the Holy Spirit to those who ask him." —Luke 11:13

Winning Thought

Winners get excited about life. Hallelujah! When atoms get excited, they leap six energy level over the norm. The key is excitement. These three virtues – joy, hope and faith - can cause excitement. You must move too when that time comes. What causes you to be excited? Because When God makes a new thing, the old becomes obsolete. Move past your failures, surge forward by faith and love.

Mission Field Testimony

We had a journey all day to get to a village in the outskirts of Nepal. It was close to the Himalayas and the journey was excruciating. I had suffered a mild bronchitis attack while climbing the mountain. In fact, I got healed that day after I received prayer from the man of God. I wanted to give up and turn back but when I saw the old women and the young women climbing with ease, I felt ashamed and decided to wing it.

When we got to the top of the mountain, I saw the glory of God. Magnificent will be an understatement. Everywhere was covered with clouds. I saw children and babies playing with freedom. We had come to visit a small church that was hidden on the mountain top to prevent being discovered and torn down by the government.

Once the service started, and we began to sing, I heard what sounded like "a rushing wind." At first, I thought the windows were open and that it was raining but it wasn't. The Holy Spirit had come in and the people started speaking in tongues. Now, mind you, these were new Christians and they had never heard about the Holy Spirit or speaking in tongues. We were all amazed and we cried that day. We saw them weeping and at the same time full of joy. They knew that something different had happened to them. They knew that the Comforter had come to assist them to live a full Christian life. It had not been easy being a Christian in Nepal but the Helper had come. Oh, glory hallelujah!

Today's Prayer

There is power in the name of Jesus to break every chain. Lord, you alone can raise army that will rise to fight battles and win victories. It's you and you alone who can do it and we thank you. Please, help me to be a part of this army, in Jesus' name. Amen.

Further Bible Reading: Proverbs 20 and 21.

Day 31

SUPERNATURAL POWER

Bible Reading

"The Lord will guarantee a blessing on everything you do and will fill your storehouses with grain. The Lord your God will bless you in the land he is giving you."
—*Deuteronomy 28:8*

Winning Thought

Winners enjoy the abundance of God's blessings. Glory to God. They love to display His supernatural power. Winners know the difference between visions and goals. Visions can be dreams and thoughts and prophetic words given to you. Things you see yourself doing. Goals are steps to carry out your visions. Both must be written down. Both must be pursued. Goals result in success. Visions without goals cannot succeed. Win in Jesus' name!

Blessings are results of God's supernatural power. And His blessings make rich, without adding sorrow.

Mission Field Testimony

I was in Rwanda in 2012. I met the widows in the Mandela Village then. I connected with them and I wrote my vision down: "I will help get water tanks for all the widows in this village." I didn't know how it would happen but I trusted in the supernatural abundance of God. I believed that God can do anything. I believed that God wants to bless people and He wants to see them prosper.

The ultimate testimony is that all the widows now have water tanks. Yes, the school has a big water tank and it's been one the greatest treasures of my life to see the joy on their faces. When I asked them to raise their hands if they had received their water tanks, ALL the women raised their hands.

I give God all the glory and it's all by His grace. YOU CAN DO ANYTHING YOU WANT because NOTHING IS IMPOSSIBLE WITH GOD.

Today's Prayer

God help me to believe that you do have supernatural power and that there's nothing impossible for you to do.

Further Bible Reading: Mark 11, 12 and 13.

CONFESSION FOR WINNERS

- God will open up doors beyond my education and my skills.
- God's favor will never run dry, never run out in my life.
- I will not be a liability to any man but be carried only by Jesus.
- God will honor the works of my hands and approve my success.
- God is a shield of protection around me.
- The Angels sent on assignment to assist me will not be hindered or stopped by anything or anyone.
- My children will work in favor all the days of their lives.
- The Lord will give me back double blessings for my years of misery.
- I will live out Psalm 24; the earth is the Lord's and everything in it.
- Also, Psalm 27:11-12; I will not fall into the hands of my enemies.
- I am taught by the Lord to live everyday to the fullness

BIOGRAPHY

The name Minister Stacy "Nkem" Egbo is synonymous with creative excellence in the Christian music community of Houston Texas, where she resides with her loving family of her husband and 5 wonderful children. The founder and leader of The Worshippers Club, a worship training ministry started in 2007, Stacy has raised worship leaders all over the world.

As an award-winning singer-songwriter, she started her ministry in a small town Enugu, Nigeria. Born to a family of 23 siblings she grew up singing gospel music amidst a family without a Christian background. How did this happen? Well, God chooses us even while we were in our mother's womb and once we accepts His call, He will work in us. At a young age of 7, she led a musical procession during the class confirmation. That launched her passion in music and since then has led Christian worshippers into the throne room of God.

After obtaining degrees in Chemistry from Anambra State University of Technology in Eastern Nigeria, she moved to the United States to pursue a career in Industrial Chemistry. She attended Texas Southern University and received a Master's Degree in Analytical Chemistry. It was while in the United States that she joined the Lakewood Church. She auditioned and was accepted in the choir. In the same year, she met her future husband, Tony Egbo, who got saved while attending Lakewood Church. Stacy moved to the suburb of Houston and started attending a Nigerian Church locally with her husband. She became the worship leader and since then has been leading worship for over 21 years in different churches.

In 2006, Stacy obtained a Bachelor's degree in Nursing and through that, the course of her life changed. During the Hurricane Katrina, God placed in Stacy's heart the passion for medical missions and using her skills to reach out to the poor and share the love of Jesus Christ. In 2007, her first medical mission to Brazil, South America changed everything. Since then Stacy has been on more 50 missions in over 26 countries.

Minister Stacy Egbo is a sought after worship leader, keynote speaker and worship trainer all over the world. Her first album "All the Nations Arise" was released in 1999, followed by 3 other albums. In

2003, a live recording at her church then, Dominion Chapel, was recorded and thousands of copies sold around the world. Later in 2014, she released another album titled "life, love and amazing grace".

She has ministered with renowned worship leaders and recording artists such as William Murphy, Ron Kenoly, William Mcdowell, Anthony Evans, Cyndi Cruise and the Lakewood Choir, Judy Jacobs, Israel Houghton, Micah Stampely and Alvin Slaughter and many others…

Stacy took a break in 2007 to help raise young worship leaders, forming the group The Worshipers Club. The group has blessed thousands of people during worship conferences and crusades. The group plans to regroup and start ministering again.

In 2011, Stacy went back to Lakewood and became a worship intern. Graduated in 2012 as a lay minister in worship, doors of ministry started opening up. Having ministered before Heads of States, crusades and conventions with massive crowds in attendance, her heart shines through for Jesus.

In 2013, Stacy was recognized in her community for the Best Gospel Star for Africa 2013. She has won other awards such as "Mother of the Year", "Community leader of the year in the Diaspora", Contemporary gospel artist of the year in the diaspora", and "Teacher of the Year award for

HISD". No award is greater than being a wife to Pastor Tony Egbo and mother to her children. She looks forward to the greatest award from her Father and Savior Jesus on the day when we will all meet Him. Thus, soul winning is a hunger that Stacy pursues as she goes around the world in missions and ministry.

Although Stacy Egbo is known all over the world for her contributions of encouraging words and worship music, she remains humble, recognizing her blessings come from God. Recently Stacy started a women's conference tagged JustDoIt, a yearly event targeted on women empowerment.

NOTE

_____

_____

_____

_____

_____

_____

_____

_____

_____

_____

NOTE

_____

_____

_____

_____

_____

_____

_____

_____

_____

_____

_____

NOTE

_____

_____

_____

_____

_____

_____

_____

_____

_____

_____

_____

NOTE

_____

_____

_____

_____

_____

_____

_____

_____

_____

_____

_____

_____

www.ingramcontent.com/pod-product-compliance
Lightning Source LLC
Chambersburg PA
CBHW070519030426

42337CB00016B/2026